THE LITTLE BOOK OF

ASTON VILLA

Independent and Unofficial

First published in 2011 by Carlton Books Publishing Group Limited

This updated edition published by OH
An Imprint of HEADLINE PUBLISHING GROUP LIMITED

1

Disclaimer:
This book has not been licensed, approved, sponsored, or endorsed by Aston Villa F.C. or any rightsholder(s) in respect of this brand.

Aston Villa F.C. is a registered trademark owned by Aston Villa Football Club Limited, Villa Park Trinity Road, Aston, Birmingham, West Midlands, B6 6HE

Cataloguing in Publication Data is available from the British Library

ISBN 978-1-03543-481-7

Compiled and written by: Dave Woodhall
Editorial: Matt Tomlinson
Designed and typset in Swiss 721 by: Stephen Cary
Project manager: Russell Porter
Production: Arlene Lestrade
Printed and bound in Dubai

MIX
Paper | Supporting responsible forestry
FSC® C104740
FSC www.fsc.org

Headline's policy is to use papers that are natural, renewable and recyclable products and made from wood grown in well-managed forests and other controlled sources. The logging and manufacturing processes are expected to conform to the environmental regulations of the country of origin.

HEADLINE PUBLISHING GROUP LIMITED
An Hachette UK Company
Carmelite House, 50 Victoria Embankment, London EC4Y 0DZ

The authorised representative in the EEA is Hachette Ireland, 8 Castlecourt Centre, Dublin 15, D15 XTP3, Ireland (email: info@hbgi.ie)

www.headline.co.uk www.hachette.co.uk

THE LITTLE BOOK OF

ASTON VILLA

Independent and Unofficial

THIRD EDITION

EDITED BY
DAVE WOODHALL

CONTENTS

INTRODUCTION

The history of Aston Villa bears striking similarities to the history of English football itself. We gave the modern game to the world in the shape of the Football League, dominated in its formative years and then sat back complacently as everyone else went shooting past us. There was a brief moment of glory some time ago when we proved that we could still compete with, and beat, all-comers but since then flattering to deceive has become an art form.

Since this book was first published we've had new owners good and bad, managers good, bad and God-like. The relegation we'd been promising for years finally happened and we tried to do it again. We've had cup finals, some of the best and worst football a Villa team has ever produced, an Academy graduate sold for £100 million and that much spent on players we could hardly give away. We've had great days when no-one was allowed into the ground and European glory nights when the sound coming out of Villa Park could be heard on the moon. And there's plenty more where that came from.

Contained herein are just a few of the many memorable statements made about the Villa. They combine to form an insight into the most historical, and infuriating, football club in the world.

CHAPTER 1

ONCE UPON A TIME IN THE MIDLANDS

Founded in 1874, Aston Villa Football Club are one of England's oldest and most successful clubs. Their story is full of colour, glory and occasional controversy...

“If there is a club in the country which deserves to be dubbed the greatest, few will deny the right of Aston Villa to share the highest niche of fame with even the most historic of other aspirants. For brilliance and for consistency of achievement, for astute management and for general alertness, the superiors of Aston Villa cannot be found.”

WILLIAM MCGREGOR, *Aston Villa committee member and founder of the Football League*

“Wanted: manager for Aston Villa Football Club, who will be required to devote his whole time under direction of the committee. Salary £100 per annum. Applications with reference must be made not later than June 23rd to Chairman of the Committee, Aston Villa Club House, 6 Witton Road, Aston.”

Newspaper advertisement: Villa received 150 applicants for the role, but committee member George Ramsay was appointed on 26 June 1886 with the title of club secretary

“Since it has been our lot to frequent football matches we have never been witness of such disgraceful scenes. If the dribbling game is to be marred by such cowardly exhibitions, the sooner football is consigned to oblivion the better for all concerned.”

Birmingham's Saturday News *on disturbances at the Villa v Preston FA Cup tie in 1888 when the cavalry were called in to restore order*

“Every year it is becoming more and more difficult for football clubs of any standing to meet their friendly engagements and even arrange friendly matches.”

The opening sentence of the letter written by **WILLIAM MCGREGOR** *to 11 other chairmen, which eventually led to the formation of the Football League, 1888*

> "STOLEN! From the Shop Window of W. Shilcock, Football Outfitter, Newtown Row, Birmingham, between the hour of 9-30 p.m. on Wednesday, the 11th September, and 7-30 a.m., on Thursday, the 12th inst., the ENGLISH CUP, the property of Aston Villa F.C."

Police poster after the original FA Cup was stolen while in Villa's care in 1895. The trophy was never recovered

“What pleasure could ladies ever have in watching a game of football on such a miserable afternoon? Would they not have been better employed at home darning socks or assisting in the housework rather than catching colds at Perry Barr?”

The Birmingham Mail *with less tact in 1896 than now*

"Never in the history of the great annual struggle for the principal trophy of Association Football has finer spectacle been seen, and such intense excitement over football game has rarely been known."

The Sporting Life *match report on 10 April 1887*

ASTON VILLA

“Without doubt the present Aston Villa team comprises the finiest body of footballers that ever stepped on to any field.”

The Sporting Life *report on 12 April 1897*

“I cannot judge the finer points of the game, but I can judge the great qualities displayed; those qualities distinctly recognized as British.”

LORD ROSEBERY *on presenting Villa with the FA Cup in 1897*

“We like to get young men and train them into our particular style. This style is difficult to describe, but we prefer skilful control of the ball, sound defence and, above all, teamwork.”

HOWARD SPENCER, *turn-of-the-century Villa full-back, captain and later director*

“Beware of the clever, sharp men who are creeping into the game.”

WILLIAM MCGREGOR *in League Football and the Men Who Made It, 1909*

“Finance is important, but we should never forget that we are not talking about a mere business. This is the Aston Villa football club, and it deserves nothing short of the best.”

Club director **FREDERICK RINDER** *during the boardroom battles of the 1920s*

“There were no rules for Pongo. Nobody knew what time he would turn up for training – ten o’clock, eleven o’clock, twelve o’clock, it made no odds. Nobody on the staff could do anything with him although I think I can claim, as the captain in his days, to be the only person able to handle him. He was a funny lad indeed.”

BILLY WALKER *recalling working with Thomas “Pongo” Waring. Despite the lack of rules, Pongo’s 226 appearances for Villa yielded 167 goals, including 10 hat-tricks and a club record 49 league goals in the 1930–31 season.*

ASTON VILLA

> "He earned the name because of his malodorous feet."

Tranmere Rovers historian **GILBERT UPTON** *on how Tranmere and Villa legend Thomas "Pongo" Waring came by his nickname*

“When Villa appoint a manager I hope the board will permit him to manage and support him.”

Sports Argus editorial on the club's decision to appoint their first manager in May 1934

ASTON VILLA

" The trouble with touring abroad with England is that everyone you meet only wants to talk about Aston Villa. "

TED DRAKE, *Arsenal and England centre-forward, in the 1930s*

“In the very first minute of the match I went tumbling and landed flat on my face. The Villa fans howled with laughter, but I think it fair to say I had the last laugh.”

TED DRAKE *on the game in which he scored seven goals at Villa Park, December 1935*

"A civic, if not a national, disaster…"

The Birmingham Mail*'s editorial column after Villa were first relegated in 1936*

“The Villa club has traditions second to none; above all, the material I have to work on possesses hereditary football ability.”

Villa manager **JIMMY HOGAN** *on his appointment in 1936*

“I’ve no time for those theories. Get the ball in the bloody net, that’s what I want.”

Villa chairman **FREDERICK NORMANSELL**
at the time Hogan was appointed

“They said we’d got to, so we said that for peace and quietness we’d give the Nazi salute. At the next place both teams gave the Nazi salute, so we went to the centre of the field and gave them two fingers and they cheered like mad.”

ERIC HOUGHTON *describes the furore surrounding Villa’s 1938 tour of Nazi Germany, when they were advised by the Foreign Office to follow local custom, and did so after a fashion*

ASTON VILLA

“A great man in every way.”

MATT BUSBY'S *tribute to Jimmy Hogan upon the former Villa manager's death in 1974*

CHAPTER 2

REVIVING A SLEEPING GIANT

Villa's fall from grace was as dramatic but sadly all-too predictable – the warning signs had been posted but there seemed little that could be done to stop the rot.

“As you got near to Villa Park, it was as if there was an army on the march. All you could see was people wearing Villa hats and scarves, carrying rattles and walking towards the ground.”

Entertainer **ALLAN RANDALL** *on Villa in the 1950s*

"Training was terribly slack. Players strolled up at any old time. Some would just walk round the track, and one used to go over the far side for a smoke."

PETER MCPARLAND, *scorer in the 1957 FA Cup Final, describes life at Villa Park in the 1950s*

“The finest coach the world had ever known. He used to say football was like a Viennese waltz, a rhapsody: one-two-three, one-two-three, pass-move-pass, pass-move-pass. We were sat there, glued to our seats, because we were so keen to learn.”

TOMMY DOCHERTY *on Jimmy Hogan, who had coached Docherty at Celtic after the war. Jimmy was invited back to Villa in 1950, aged 68, to help coach the youth team where he stayed until retiring in 1959.*

“Everything Hogan did was geared around ball control and passing. When Jimmy came to Villa, he was revolutionary… He would get you doing step-overs, little turns and twists on the ball and everything you did was to make you comfortable on the ball.”

RON ATKINSON *on one of Hogan's apprentices at Villa bewteen 1956–59*

“ I played with Ron in about a hundred reserve games. And, according to Ron, he was Man of the Match in at least 99 of them. ”

Former Villa player **DENNIS JACKSON** *on his contemporary Ron Atkinson*

"He invented the banana shot. Trouble was, he was trying to shoot straight."

RON ATKINSON *returns the compliment with regard to Jackson's shooting abilities*

ASTON VILLA

" The club had grown fat and lazy on its old traditions and the decay was eating at the once-solid foundations. "

DANNY BLANCHFLOWER *requested transfer in 1954*

“They were lovely men, but they were totally unsuited to running a club like the Villa. They were too old; football was changing, and they weren’t up to it.”

Ex-manager **TOMMY CUMMINGS** *pinpoints the reason for the Villa’s failings in the 1960s. It was the directors…*

“ The big myth of British soccer – that Aston Villa are still a major force. **”**

The Birmingham Post*'s sorry comment on the Villa Park situation, 1964*

“If you keep buying Third Division players, where do you think you’ll end up?”

Ex-Villa player and broadcaster **LARRY CANNING**
on Villa’s slide during the 1960s

“In the end, it was solved by the directors of the Villa themselves, who sent the longest telegram in history… It was the most ambiguous telegram and we had no idea what it meant, but Brian Evans, who chaired the meeting, said ‘I don’t care what it says, just go out and say it says Aston Villa is up for sale.’”

JOHN RUSSELL *recalling when around 1,000 disgruntled Villa supporters packed the Digbeth Civic Hall on 21 November 1968*

“I am sure that influential people in Birmingham, the sort of people who controlled things, decided a change was needed. They couldn’t be seen to be involved publicly, but their influence was there.”

ERIC WOODWARD, *who became Villa commercial manager, commenting on events that led to the board’s mass resignation in 1968*

“You could write your name in the dust, window frames were rotting, the smell of failure and imminent financial ruin hung in the air.”

DOUG ELLIS

“There was something about it all that made an instant impression. It just hit me. I went home thinking, ‘I hope I get an opportunity to join that football club.’”

BRIAN LITTLE *on the time he first visited Villa Park as a 15-year-old hopeful in 1969*

“Aston Villa will play in the European Cup one day.”

TOMMY DOCHERTY'S *prophetic parting shot after his dismissal as manager, January 1970*

"When the visiting team went out to look at the pitch at two o'clock, there would already be more people in the ground than they were used to seeing at kick-off time."

Former captain **BRIAN GODFREY** *on Villa's prodigious Third Division crowds in the 1970s*

“Every good team has a strong centre. I’d look round. Goalkeeper, Jim Cumbes. I’d think, ‘What time did you get in last night?’ Centre-half, Chris Nicholl. In the toilet putting his contact lenses in. Central midfield, Bruce Rioch. Shaking like a leaf. Centreforward, Sammy Morgan. Next to Chris putting his contact lenses in. What chance did I have?”

VIC CROWE, *Villa manager of the early 1970s*

“We were playing away, and we’d taken this 15-year-old apprentice with us. As was the custom, a whisky bottle was passed round. Players took a drink, then when they’d gone onto the pitch Vic Crowe took a big swig. The apprentice asked him why and he replied, ‘Son, when you’re manager of this club you’ll know why.’”

JIM CUMBES, *goalkeeper in the early 1970s*

CHAPTER 3

GLORY & PAIN

Under Ron Saunders, Villa not only became champions of England, but champions of Europe... but those heady days were soon in the rearview mirror as the club nosedived again.

“With 110% from each and every one of the players and your usual tremendous vocal backing, I am sure we can get the right result.”

RON SAUNDERS’ *programme notes invariably contained this or a similarly rousing phrase*

“I hopped in the taxi to Glasgow Airport with one thought in my mind – where on earth was Aston Villa?”

ANDY GRAY *describes the journey that led to him signing for Villa in 1975*

“EVEN GRECIAN 2000 CAN’T STOP GRAY.”

A supporter’s banner at the 1977 League Cup Final, which finished 0–0. Villa won the cup after a second replay when Gray was absent

“We often played golf together and he always beat me, then one day I won for the first time. Two weeks later, I was sold.”

Then club captain **CHRIS NICHOLL** *on why Ron Saunders offloaded him during the summer of 1977*

“My team won’t freeze in the white heat of Anfield.”

RON SAUNDERS, *true to form as ever*

“I defy any football devotee not to sense that this would be a perfect setting for the championship trophy.”

The Evening Mail*'s* **RAY MATTS**, *standing on the Villa Park pitch on the eve of the 1980–81 season*

“He made me captain by saying, ‘Right, you lead ’em out.’”

DENNIS MORTIMER *on how he was chosen by Ron Saunders to become Villa’s most successful captain of all time*

“Do you want to bet against us?”

RON SAUNDERS, *after Villa were beaten in a vital championship decider against Ipswich in April 1981. Ipswich collapsed, losing four of their last five games, allowing Villa to win their seventh Division One crown, but their only top-flight title of the past 115 years*

“Let me be the first to congratulate Aston Villa.”

Radio Two announcer **BRYON BUTLER** *as results elsewhere meant that Villa became league champions, May 1981*

"I grew up being a Villa fan in the 70s when Ron Saunders was in charge. He built an unbelievable team. He won the League Cup twice and built an incredible team that I was fortunate to come and watch here. To win the league in 1981 with only 14 players – six or seven made 42 appearances and played every minute of every game – was incredible."

DEAN SMITH

Paying tribute to Ron Saunders after his death in 2019

“I have always maintained that I want to spend the rest of my managerial career with Aston Villa. But the situation means the club have less confidence in me… I am paid to be the manager, not the office boy.”

RON SAUNDERS

“There’s a battle going on, but I am not leaving this football club.”

RON SAUNDERS, *to Dennis Mortimer, the day before his resignation in February 1982*

“Shaw, Williams, prepared to venture down the left. There’s a good ball in for Tony Morley. Oh, it must be and it is! It’s Peter Withe!”

The legendary **BRIAN MOORE’S** *epic commentary on the 1982 European Cup winning goal for Villa*

ASTON VILLA

“This is the shin that won the European Cup.”

PETER WITHE, *rolling up his trouser leg in front of celebrating Villa fans at the subsequent civic reception*

“Goal of the Season? No chance. Goal of the Month? Not a hope. It was only Goal of the Game because there were no others.”

Local journalist **ROB BISHOP** *on Peter Withe's European Cup winner in his book,* The Road to Rotterdam

“The hardest part of captaining that team was tossing the coin and picking up the trophies.”

DENNIS MORTIMER, *League Championship- and European Cup-winning captain*

“When you’ve been given a free transfer by Southport and Barrow, you learn to live with disappointment.”

PETER WITHE *after being dropped from the England squad in 1982*

“ The club will not accept constant failure. **”**

Chairman **DOUG ELLIS** *on his reasons for sacking Tony Barton for finishing 10th in 1983–84. Three years later, Villa were relegated…*

“I promised you in 1969 that no one person or group of people would ever be allowed to control the club… I have never had a controlling shareholding in Aston Villa and have no wish to do so.”

DOUG ELLIS, *when fighting unsuccessfully to retain his seat on the board in 1979*

“When he was recovering in hospital, one of our sons said the words, ‘Doug Ellis’, and the heart monitor went shooting up. All the nurses came rushing in.”

ROSINA BARTON, *wife of former Villa manager Tony, describes her husband’s recovery from a heart attack in 1985*

ASTON VILLA

> “Would anyone argue against the assertion that the Trinity Road entrance of Villa Park has more pomp and style than that of any other ground?”

SIMON INGLIS *in* The Football Grounds of England and Wales

“ ‘Was that the season when you came home one night and said you were never going there again, even if they sent a chauffeur-driven limousine to collect you?’

‘Yes.’

‘Then you went there the next Saturday?’ ”

A conversation between Villa supporter **PETER ALDRIDGE** *and his wife recorded in* Heroes & Villains *fanzine*

"The whole club needs restructuring. The youth policy is not good enough, the scouting system is not good enough, the team is a shambles and I have come to sort it out."

GRAHAM TAYLOR *upon his appointment as Villa manager in the summer of 1987*

“You don’t get this at Birmingham City.”

DOUG ELLIS *prior to a recital by violin virtuoso Nigel Kennedy at the Villa AGM*

“A swarming mass of humanity: 20,000 or more voices screaming out their support for the claret and blue.”

Villa fan **SIMON PAGE** *describes the pre-Taylor Report Holte End*

“You got yourselves into this f*****g mess. You can get yourselves out of it.”

GRAHAM TAYLOR, *when Villa were 2–0 down at halftime in an FA Cup third-round game at Crewe, January 1989. He then walked out of the dressing room. Villa won 3–2…*

“We’ve signed enough injury prone has-beens.”

Anonymous Villa supporter quoted in the Wolverhampton Express & Star *when the club bought Paul McGrath in 1989*

“One of the all-time greats. Someone to compare with Bobby Moore.”

JACK CHARLTON *on McGrath*

“Twenty-seven years old, choice health, good knees, world-class agent. There was no way I could fail.”

TONY CASCARINO *describes his record-breaking move to Villa in 1990*

ASTON VILLA

“I am a human being. I support Aston Villa, but I am still a human being.”

JOHN TAYLOR, *prospective Conservative parliamentary candidate for Cheltenham, after being racially abused by fellow Tories, 1990*

“FOR GOD’S SAKE GO DOCTOR JO...”

The Evening Mail, *reacting to defeat in time-honoured fashion by calling for the dismissal of manager Dr Josef Venglos, April 1991*

"If he'd come a few years later he might have done better because by then the European ideas were better accepted… English football was always going to go the European way, and Jo was the start of it."

Former Villa midfielder **PAUL BIRCH** *offers a different slant on Venglos' time at Villa Park*

“If that lad makes a First Division footballer, then I’m Mao Tse Tung.”

TOMMY DOCHERTY *on Dwight Yorke after his Villa debut in 1990. Eight years later he was sold to Manchester United for £12.6 million*

“I’ll never be able to achieve what Tommy Docherty did and take Aston Villa into the Third Division and Manchester United into the Second Division.”

RON ATKINSON

"Someone asked me last week if I miss the Villa. I said, 'No, I live in one.'"

DAVID PLATT *after his record-breaking transfer to Bari, 1991*

“As a youngster I was one of Villa’s keenest supporters. I played there and I always believed that one day I would return as manager.”

RON ATKINSON

“I just wanted to give them some technical advice. I told them the game had started.”

RON ATKINSON *explaining why he moved from the stand to the dug-out during a game with Sheffield United, 1993*

“People in this game don’t realise how lucky they are. You drive to the ground, play a few five-a-sides, then have lunch. It’s wonderful, enjoyable fun.”

ATKINSON *again, speaking when Villa were pushing for the Premiership title, 1993*

“I always make sure I write ‘Atkinson, D.’ on the team-sheet. Sometimes I wonder if I’m making a mistake.”

RON ATKINSON *on the inconsistencies of his namesake Dalian*

“It's nice that Terry (Cooper) has his son playing for us and you've got your son here.”

Blues chief executive **KARREN BRADY**, *getting her Atkinsons mixed up*

“ Once Tony Daley opens his legs, you’re in trouble. **”**

Former Leeds manager **HOWARD WILKINSON**

“You wouldn’t have done that if Eamonn Deacy was playing.”

Voice from the Holte End as Ruud Gullit strode majestically through the Villa defence for Chelsea, 1996. Former Villa defender Deacy was not known for his cultured approach to the beautiful game…

CHAPTER 4

THE TIMES THEY ARE CHANGIN'

Villa moved towards the new millennium with a mixture of dread and optimism...

ASTON VILLA

" Our shares are a good bet in the short, medium and long term. "

Villa finance director **MARK ANSELL** *after the club floated on the Stock Exchange in 1997, with shares at £11 each. Five years later they were trading at just over £1*

“The game has been tailored to the wine-bar fraternity. The culture has gradually been eradicated.”

Classical violinist and Villa supporter **NIGEL KENNEDY**, *1997*

“This is my field of dreams.”

STAN COLLYMORE *on Villa Park pitch after signing in May 1997*

“Stan’s a lovely man, a lovely lad. He’s just made one or two bad decisions.”

BRIAN LITTLE *on his record signing, and nemesis, Mr Collymore*

“How does Stan Collymore change a light bulb? He holds it in the air and the world revolves around it.”

Joke doing the Villa Park rounds during another of Collymore's absences

“We knew how close we were to being a real force, but the more we tried to make that leap, the further away we seemed to be. Alex Ferguson said Villa was the team he could see coming through.”

GARETH SOUTHGATE *on Villa's maddeningly close brush with the elite under Brian Little*

“I’d like to play for an Italian club, like Barcelona...”

MARK DRAPER, *who later joined English club Southampton*

“The accelerator’s position meant my right knee was giving me grief.”

Diminutive full-back **ALAN WRIGHT***, explaining why he was selling his £50,000 Ferrari, 1997*

“We spent enough money; we just bought the wrong players.”

Former assistant manager **ALLAN EVANS** *explaining Villa's fall from grace during 1997–98*

“The chairman of Brighton wouldn’t recognize Gareth Barry if he was stood on Brighton beach in the team strip, with a seagull on his head and a ball in his hand.”

JOHN GREGORY *in response to claims that Brighton made Barry the player he is and were worthy of a £2.5m compensation payment*

“There’s an aura about this club, a sense of history and tradition. Even the name is beautifully symmetrical, with five letters in each word.”

JOHN GREGORY *waxes lyrical, 1998*

"There is a very good living to be made at Villa Park, provided the club never looks in danger of getting relegated."

Wolverhampton Express & Star *reporter* **MARTIN SWAIN** *sums up the "comfort zone" mentality of Villa during the late-1990s*

“Stress is a player at Rochdale with a family to bring up and a contract expiring at the end of the season.”

JOHN GREGORY, *commenting on Stan Collymore's admission to the Priory Hospital suffering from stress, 1999*

“I’ve said to him, I wish I was you, Stan. I wish I was on the money you’re earning. I wish I had your lifestyle. And most of all I wish I had your talent because with it, I’d have been the first name in the England team.”

GREGORY *tries a slightly more conciliatory approach towards his errant forward*

“You can’t be sure he will be taken on by a club anywhere. Unless it’s some Outer Mongolian outfit that has been locked away from news, television and society for 10 years.”

The Nottingham Post *after a report that Forest were considering taking* **COLLYMORE** *off Villa’s hands in 1999. They didn’t…*

“The fans wanted Ginger Spice in basque and suspenders. I gave them Norah Batty in wrinkled stockings.”

JOHN GREGORY *on how he managed his resources*

“There are 92 league teams, but whenever a pantomime like this happens, you know who one of the clubs will be.”

A Heroes & Villains *fanzine editorial during one of Villa's many transfer wrangles in the 1990s*

"They never cease to think up ways to embarrass you."

Heard from the crowd during one of the club's more ludicrous attempts to whip up pre-match fervour as yet another fanfare sounded out to announce the arrival of the teams onto the pitch

“My addictions are always there, waiting there for me. They’re doing press-ups outside my door.”

PAUL MERSON, *1999*

ASTON VILLA

“To compete week-in, week-out against the Man Us, Arsenals, Liverpools and Chelseas says a lot about the little team from Birmingham that plays so big!”

Programme for a pre-season tournament in New York, 1999

“There’s something curious about the relationship between Coventry and Villa. We don’t particularly dislike them. But blimey, do they hate us!”

JOHN GREGORY *on the vagaries of West Midlands football, 1999*

“I personally think referees should be wired up to a couple of electrodes and they should be allowed to make three mistakes before you run 50,000 volts through their genitals.”

GREGORY *during his run-ins with referees at the start of the 1999–2000 season*

“Too many of us were playing in the comfort zone, where it doesn’t hurt enough if we lost. Sometimes I wonder if we care enough.”

PAUL MERSON, *talking about Villa’s underachieving side of the late-1990s*

“Villa always give the impression that they’re happier being sixth in the table than second. Because they can get to sixth without much effort, but when they’re second they have to try to be first.”

Holy Trinity *fanzine editor* **STEVE WHITEHOUSE**
expands on the “comfort zone” mentality

“There’s as much chance of a recession as there is of Aston Villa winning the league.”

Villa fan **MERVYN KING** *on being appointed Governor of the Bank of England in 1999. Villa were top of the league at the time…*

“Why all the fuss over Prince William becoming an Aston Villa fan? At least he didn't choose to support Manchester United like everybody else in Berkshire.”

Sun columnist **RICHARD LITTLEJOHN**, *2000*

“Carbone retired with the dignity of a three-year-old being led past the sweet counter at Tesco, flinging down his headband and kicking the trainer’s bucket.”

The Guardian’s **DAVID LACEY** *on Benito Carbone’s histrionics during the 2000 FA Cup semi-final versus Bolton*

"That man Boateng must have an incredibly hard chin."

Paul Gascoigne's agent, **MEL STEIN***, after his player broke an arm on George Boateng's face, 2000*

CHAPTER 5

ONWARDS AND UPWARDS

After a roller-coaster existence for so long, Villa enjoyed a period of relative calm, with the odd high here and there...

“I’m a much better manager than when I started, but not half as good as I will be.”

JOHN GREGORY’S *mission statement, 2000*

“It was beautiful. The sensitivity from everyone he met in Birmingham really impressed David.”

CHANTELLE STANLEY, *David Ginola's agent, shortly after the French winger signed for Villa in 2000*

“You wonder if this city will ever run out of grey paint.”

DAVID GINOLA *didn't take long to be less than impressed with Birmingham*

“Young Gareth Barry, you know, he’s young.”

The ever-astute **KEVIN KEEGAN** *on the qualities of Gareth Barry*

"Aston Villa always seem to have problems taking the final step towards being a really big club."

GRAHAM TAYLOR *on his return to Villa Park as manager of Watford in 2001*

"I was in hospital with instructions not to have any visitors for 24 hours. I awoke to find Ron Atkinson at the end of my bed saying, 'Sorry, I'm late, but I had to walk round the hospital three times before anybody recognised me.'"

TV presenter **GARY NEWBON**

“The ever-growing number of spokesmen, for the ever-growing number of Villa protest groups.”

MARTIN SWAIN'S *sardonic look at the unique nature of Villa supporter politics, February 2002*

“I think they’re great.”

His Royal Highness **PRINCE WILLIAM**

“I know almost every player by name already. I play a lot of Championship Manager and Gareth Barry is always a good buy. Hopefully he is just as good in real life.”

JOEY GUDJONSSON *on signing for Villa in January 2003*

“All around I see hope fading. And you ask any football fan – a life without hope is a life not worth living.”

Local historian and Villa supporter **CARL CHINN**
in an interview with The Times, *March 2003*

ASTON VILLA

“The vast majority of Mr Gregory’s transfer dealings were unfortunate. A vast fortune in transfer fees and wages were committed to players who in the main did not match up to expectations.”

The Hodgson Report into the business workings of Aston Villa, summer 2003

"John's resignation is sad. It was most unexpected but has been amicable."

Chairman **DOUG ELLIS** *reflects on John Gregory's decision to quit as Vila boss in January 2002 after four years in the hot seat.*

“There are fundamental problems at Aston Villa that are preventing it from becoming a top four club.”

GRAHAM TAYLOR *upon resigning as manager, after just a few months back at the club in 2003*

“It’s a club that I want to turn around and make it big again and I’m going to try and do that. I’m so happy. You have start putting the club back where it belongs – at the very top, get the crowds in and play good football and I’m looking forward to giving it my best shot.”

DAVID O’LEARY *is named as new Villa boss in May 2003*

" O'Leary was never anything less than courteous, friendly and, above all, professional. But he did appear to have a secretive, cynical, perhaps spiteful, side to his nature. "

Leeds supporter **GARY EDWARDS***, writing about David O'Leary's time at Elland Road*

ASTON VILLA

“Finest hour: marrying on the pitch. It made Match of the Day.”

Villa mascot **BELLA***, when she and fellow furry creature, Hercules the Lion, got married and the ceremony was shown on national TV*

“A top-six place doesn’t come cheap. I don’t want a 22-man squad but I’m asking for 18, which is not excessive.”

DAVID O’LEARY

reflecting on the lack of funding for transfers after Villa had let go of 13 players. Despite a poor start to the 2003–04 season, Villa finished in 6th position, missing out on a UEFA Cup place only on goal difference.

“I’m ambitious and I want to manage at the top but I’ve never broken a contract in my life and, if there’s no money this summer, I won’t spit my dummy out.”

DAVID O’LEARY *and his realistic outlook, April 2004*

“With my Jamaican hand on my Ethiopian heart, the African heart deep in my Brummie chest. And I chant, Aston Villa, Aston Villa, Aston Villa… I don’t have an identity crisis.”

From “Knowing Me” by Rastafarian Brummie poet **BENJAMIN ZEPHANIAH**

“I’m big on Aston Villa because the name is just so sweet. Other clubs are like ‘Arrrrsenal’ or ‘Maaaan United’ but Aston Villa sounds like a lovely spa.”

Film star **TOM HANKS** *explaining why he’s a Villa supporter, 2004*

ASTON VILLA

“As a boy, I found that the exotic Englishness of such names oddly resembled those of Crystal Palace, Aston Villa, West Bromwich Albion and Charlton Athletic – all more exciting than the Knights of the Round Table in their silly tin armour, by far.”

Poet and author **CHRIS WALLACE-CRABBE**

from Australian newspaper The Age, *2004*

“The few trees through the corner gap are beginning to green and beyond them the M6, the world of nowhere, the world of coming from and going to, a perpetual conveyor belt.”

From “The Team in My Head”
by poet and Villa fan **DAVID HART**

“Strikers wanted.”

Written on a whiteboard at Villa's training ground at the end of 2004–05, when the side managed just 45 league goals

“I'm just sad. But you move on with life and I just wish Aston Villa all the very best.”

DAVID O'LEARY *leaves Villa, July 2006*

CHAPTER 6

A BRAVE NEW WORLD

Ahead of a what could be an exciting new era, there would be difficult days before brightness returned to Villa Park...

“I want a life of good sport, good people and the competition that goes with it. I’m here to try to get something accomplished.”

New Villa owner **RANDY LERNER** *on his motivation*

“I’m still claret and blue through and through. I’m just desperate for us to win.”

Former Villa supremo **DOUG ELLIS**

"I realise expectations are pretty high. I'm petrified! It's a great challenge and I'm raring to go but I have to prove myself and show I can do the job."

MARTIN O'NEILL *takes over at the Villa, August 2006*

“Everybody is well aware of the history of the club and while trying to restore it to those glory days is a long way away, why not try? It’s a quarter of a century since they won the European Cup and that’s a long way away at this minute.”

O’NEILL *recognises the scale of the task ahead…*

“As a kid you want to play every minute of every game – that’s what you dream about.”

GABRIEL AGBONLAHOR

“You could be looking at him becoming one of Villa’s great players. He’s already played over 300 games and he’s only 25.”

MARTIN O’NEILL *on skipper Gareth Barry*

“Martin O’Neill is a legend. You never hear a player say a bad word about him – even when they are not in the team. You feel like he wants to know the players as well as he can, and he knows how to help each player.”

STILIYAN PETROV

“He wanted more than Randy Lerner could give him.”

MARTIN LAURSEN

Former Villa captain commenting after O'Neill's shock resignation just five days before the start of the season, August 2010

“For the life I’ve lived in football, I will always be incredibly grateful. For the opportunity this crazy thing that happened in my life has given me, I also feel grateful in a strange kind of way. This crazy thing, somehow, has touched people and I want to try to channel this in a positive way. This will be the greatest challenge of my life.”

STYLIAN PETROV *announces his retirement from football on Villa’s official website after his acute Leukaemia diagnosis, 2013*

“Many Premier League clubs could do without the distraction of the FA Cup if they were being honest.”

In January 2014, **PAUL LAMBERT** *angers Villa fans, desperate for silverware*

“I never decried the FA Cup in any shape or form. I never demeaned the competition. I respect its history. I put out the strongest team I could do to try to win the game. The FA Cup is a brilliant competition, and everybody wants to do well in it.”

LAMBERT *backtracks quickly to stem the vitriol…*

“I relish the challenge of trying to take the club where it wants to go and needs to be – and try to turn around the misfortune we seem to have had over the past few years.”

In October 2016, ex-Blues boss **STEVE BRUCE** *becomes Villa's sixth manager in 12 months…*

“I am like a lot of the supporters – I can’t believe what I’m watching. I have never known it so low at Aston Villa. Both the club and its supporters are at such a low ebb. Somewhere along the line the feeling around the club, with the owner wanting to sell and not being able to, has crept into the dressing room. It is like a slow death in football terms.”

Former boss **GRAHAM TAYLOR** *shares his thoughts on BBC Sport in 2017*

“The guy who is being questioned… unfortunately, it sums up the society we are in at the moment. There’s no respect for anyone. I find the whole thing hugely disrespectful.”

STEVE BRUCE *reacts to having a cabbage thrown at him at Villa Park. October 2018 – he was sacked shortly after…*

"Devastated, just heard the news about Sir Doug Ellis, absolute gentleman to me throughout my career my thoughts and prayers are with Heidi and his family."

PAUL MCGRATH *shares his sadness at the passing of former chairman Dough Ellis in October 2018*

“I cannot help but feel how lucky I was in this incident. It could have been so much worse had the supporter had some sort of weapon.”

JACK GREALISH *in March 2019 after being attacked by a Birmingham City fan at St Andrew's*

“I told him on Friday. We were in the physio room with John McGinn and a couple of the medical staff for an hour and I asked, ‘Who should be captain?’ They were throwing a few names around, before I said to Jack, ‘You’re captain tomorrow.’ He had a big smile on his face, and it would have been a proud moment for him because, like me, he’s a Villa fan and was brought up a Villa fan. To captain your team and score a goal like he did topped off a great day.”

DEAN SMITH *reveals how he informed Villa boyhood fan Grealish he was going to skipper the side in March 2019*

“Ollie has developed into one of the most sought-after strikers in the country and we are looking forward to seeing him show his great qualities in an Aston Villa shirt. He is a hugely determined character who has both the ability and personality to succeed at the highest level.”

DEAN SMITH *tells the* Birmingham Mail *how happy he is to have Ollie Watkins on board in September 2020*

“It was obviously a difficult few months because I have been an Aston Villa fan for my whole life, but in the end it was something I couldn’t say no to.”

JACK GREALISH *speaks about his £100m to Manchester City in August 2021*

“It’s a club that is so close to my heart and I definitely hope to go back there. That’s always been in my mind. Ashley Young has done it and I want to do the same, 100 per cent.”

JACK GREALISH *on the possibility of returning to Vila Park one day…*

“You can’t imagine how hard it was for me to leave. I went for a run in the morning, a load of people took photographs of me and it was all on social [media] that I was staying. I came back and had to address all the players and staff. There were about 70 people there. I spoke for about a minute and a half, then I had to stop because I had a lump in my throat and was crying. I was a bit surprised by some of the backlash when I left. I'd never want a toxic relationship with anyone there. I owe everything to them, and I wouldn't be at City without Villa. ”

JACK GREALISH

"The board would like to sincerely thank Dean for his many excellent achievements, on and off the pitch, during this time. Everyone knows how much Aston Villa means to Dean and his family. He has represented the club with distinction and dignity – universally liked and respected by everybody associated with Aston Villa."

Chief Executive **CHRISTIAN PURSLOW** *on Dean Smith's emotional exit from Villa Park in November 2021*

" No-one will ever compare, the real GOAT (greatest of all time). "

JACK GREALISH *reacts to Dean Smith's exit on X, November 2021*

“I just thought for someone who gave so much to the club, he would have been given a little bit more time.”

Former Villa defender **MICAH RICHARDS** *comments on Smith's sacking during BBC's Match of the Day*

"Aston Villa is a club with a rich history and tradition in English football and I am immensely proud to become its new head coach."

STEVEN GERRARD *on his appointment as Smith's successor in November 2021*

“Aston Villa Football Club can confirm that Head Coach Steven Gerrard has left the club with immediate effect. We would like to thank Steven for his hard work and commitment and wish him well for the future.”

Official club statement on the end of Gerrard's unhappy 11 months at Villa

"Aston Villa is delighted to announce the appointment of Unai Emery as the club's new head coach!"

Aston Villa's official website announces Emery's arrival in October 2022

“He is a football encyclopaedia.”

Villarreal midfielder **ETIENNE CAPOUE** *heaps praise on his former boss Emery*

“Between everybody, we are going to share and achieve our identity and style. We want every supporter to be proud of us.”

UNAI EMERY *on AVFC official's website, November 2022*

“I’m looking forward to being there with our supporters, I’m wishing to feel them push, the atmosphere. To play at home, for me, it’s so important to create a big atmosphere with our supporters helping us.”

UNAI EMERY

" It's a very special day. It's our dream, we started the season to be here. We've had injuries but the team was always focused. It's fantastic. "

UNAI EMERY *after Manchester City's win over Tottenham confirms a top four Premier League finish in May 2024*

“To play Champions League is the best. Nobody expected us to be there but we believed in ourselves and believed in our dream. It was hard, but the achievement is amazing.”

LUCAS DIGNE *shares his joy on Instagram*

“We are Champions League. A historic season and an amazing achievement. Thanks to Unai, the whole squad and everyone at Aston Villa. Can’t wait for next season.”

HRH PRINCE WILLIAM *on X in May 2024*

“Wild. Madness. It was a bit crazy but then the manager started talking about Wednesday.”

MORGAN ROGERS *after Villa's memorable 1–0 win over Bayern Munich in the 2024–25 UICL phase in October 2024*

> “Surreal – the atmosphere, the occasion, playing one of the biggest teams in world and competing like this. It’s all been a bit mad, that’s how quick football can change. I’ve always believed in myself. Be patient and the time will come. Luckily I found a manager who believed in me. I was probably in my shell when I came, trying to fit in. He gives me that confidence and belief in my ability.”

More from **MORGAN ROGERS**, *speaking to TNT Sports after the Bayern win*

“It’s unreal to be fair. This is the loudest Villa Park that I’ve heard since I joined the club, that’s for sure, it was hurting my ears at some point. It’s a club that is moving forward. It’s the main reason why I stay in this football club. I love playing here, I love the fans, this is a win for them.”

EMILO MARTINEZ *on TNT Sports after Villa’s 1–0 win over Bayern*

“We have to continue dreaming to achieve our individual and collective objectives… this is something positive, because you have to try to set your objectives as high as possible, like our dreams, and to work hard to get it.”

UNAI EMERY, *living the dream as Villa head towards a top-8 finish in the league phase of the Champions League, January 2025*

> "It's our year for the FA Cup."

EVERY VILLA SUPPORTER,

every January